MW01488155

Graffiti

scribbles from different sides of the street

Alene Snodgrass

Praise for *Graffiti*

"This is a beautiful and potent call to live a life that matters — from someone who's lived it. Alene calls us to think and live differently — why are we so afraid of "different"? We need to learn to embrace the discomfort that causes us to grow, and this book will help you. I was challenged by it."

-- JEFF GOINS, *author, Wrecked: When a Broken World Slams into Your Comfortable Life*

"Graffiti: Scribbles from Different Sides of the Street challenges readers to step up, step out, and make way for new marks on our soul."

-- AMY L. SULLIVAN, *blogger, finding God-sized ways to give in everyday*

"Alene's compassion and love for the "less fortunate" is contagious. Her work in the inner city reaches far and wide as she reaches out to touch those that many have forgotten about. Her book will surely encourage you to become all God desires for you to be and to do! One of the amazing qualities that Alene possesses is the ability to lift the "down and out" person up to a level of dignity and self worth. As you read this book, God will surely light a fire in you to help others as never before."

-- DEBRA GEORGE, *author and speaker*

© Alene Snodgrass. 2012.
alenesnodgrass.com

Graffiti by Alene Snodgrass.
Published in the United States of America.

All rights reserved solely by the author.

. .

Cover Design by:

Blake Snodgrass
www.AnchorMediaSolutions.com

You are welcome to use a short excerpt of this book for review
purposes.

For information or questions, please contact
alene@alenesnodgrass.com.

Table of Contents

Introduction

A few years ago God began wrecking my heart for serving "the least of these." I had no clue where to go or what to do. My argument with God was much like, *"God I'm serving your people and teaching so much in the church I have no time to serve anywhere else. And besides, I wouldn't even know what to do or where to go."* My heart ached because I knew God was doing something new, but I had no idea how to step into it.

One morning, as I set out for the day I prayed, "God I have no idea where you are calling me to serve, so will you just put someone in my path that I can bless."

I had to run into the mall to meet my daughter and as I headed down a small hallway I noticed a few homeless men sitting on the bench, cold and wet. Instantly, my heart knew I was to bless these men. Luckily, I had read Jen Hatmaker's book Interrupted and she explained how the homeless just want to be acknowledged and talked to just like you would talk to anybody else. My heart was beating fast. I knew this was the opportunity I had prayed for.

As I came down the hallway I walked over to the bench where the men were and said, "Hi! How are you doing today?" And with that I froze. I froze! Not another word came out of my mouth. I just stood there looking like a buffoon I'm quite sure!

I didn't know anything about being homeless. My mind couldn't picture ghetto. The curiosity within me wanted to know about the streets. And inside my head these thoughts raced:

Alene, say something! You know whatever you say and do it's as if you are doing it for Jesus, and here you stand speechless. Say something!

But I couldn't. Not one other thing came out of my mouth. What word did I have that could comfort this man's soul? What did we share in common for conversation? I hung my head low and turned and walked away. The screaming thoughts in my head were intense:

Alene, seriously! God provides you with an opportunity to love others and you just stand there. Jesus, I'm so sorry. Jesus, you were there and I missed an opportunity to serve you. I'm so sorry!

While I continued to beat myself up and remind myself how disappointed Jesus must be in me, one of the men hollered out:

"Ma'am, you need to know I love you!"

Others around might have been wondering what was going on, and you might be thinking the same thing. But let me tell you the peace that came over me when that man spoke out, it was as if Jesus were trying to tell me:

It's alright. I know this is all new to you. So you froze – I still love you. I'm so proud of you for stepping out!

That was the first encounter of me trying to step out into this new place Jesus was leading me. It wasn't pretty. It was awkward. Was I successful? It would seem a big NO would be the answer; however, I'd say "yes." Because I stepped out and tried, I was successful.

Your journey is all about the steps you take in obedience, baby steps at first. I've taken many more since that day and with each scary step, God blesses me abundantly! If you are reading this book, chances are God is stirring something new within your heart. Be brave. Be courageous. There is an incredible journey ahead for you as you head down a different street.

It's a journey that will surprise you with twists and turns. This journey, you can be sure, will leave graffiti scribbles all over your soul. This is a journey that you will surely not want to miss! You will progress forward with each brave step you take.

One day I ran in to another homeless soul. Feeling a little braver, I carried on a face-to-face conversation. And to my surprise we had much in common, as you'll read in the pages ahead. Although there were commonalities, we came from different sides of the street.

The graffiti scribbled on our hearts was painted the same, but with different visible colors – some soft pastels with some loud primary colors. But somewhere between those two different sides of the street with all our graffiti, there was a lot of common ground. It was a beautiful journey that led our paths to cross, while God beautifully orchestrated the scribbles of our heart that resembled . . .

Graffiti.

Unique Journeys

Do you love a good story? Oh how I do! Especially that story where the victim is down and then miraculously, through God's mercies, raises themselves up to move on. But the best part of those stories is hearing the personal testimony of how God worked and moved. I don't want to hear a story just to hear a story. No, I want to learn from a story and be empowered.

That's where you and I come in. You see, we are on unique journeys. You and I were raised differently. We probably live on different sides of the street. We walk different paths. You and I have even gone through incredible hardships; we've handled them differently and prevailed in our own unique ways.

Your life story is scribbled out each day as you live out that journey. For some of you, your journey has been free of pain and neglect, while others of you have struggled with abandonment and abuse. There's no guarantee for any journey – yours or mine. A life story can change from one minute to the next. One thing is for certain though, no matter who you are – rich or poor, black or white, employed or jobless -- you can't write the ending of your story before it is lived out.

With your last breath your story is finished. Do you wonder if your story will reflect the love you dared to give? Your heart will determine the pages of your life that will outlast you. If you can grasp that graffiti comes in many colors and is visible on many different streets, you will leave inspiring pages of love and hope on your side of the street. Graffiti? It's the scribbles of story and love that God intertwines upon your heart.

What about your story? Will it ever be heard? Or will you choose to keep it silent? I pray that you will choose to voice your heart and let your story be heard. It doesn't matter what you've been through, your silent message needs to be heard by somebody. If you think your story is not good enough, I challenge you to think about that silent thought and voice, "Why?" If you think your story is too much for others to handle or you're afraid to scribble it down, I ask you: why?

It's in telling your story that you will find the freedom that you are longing for. Once the thoughts, truths, and circumstances are out in the open, you will gain the empowerment you need to move on. Satan's lies cannot grow once they are exposed to the Light. He tricks us and stifles us from exposing the truth because he knows we become stronger when the truth prevails.

I'm excited to share *Graffiti* with you. It's a story of how God wove my story together with a brother's story from the street. As I challenged him to write and share, he gained confidence and worth. He began to realize his story and life mattered. I began to see that whether you're living on the street or in suburban America, God has a unique purpose for each one. Through my friend's scribbles, I could see a bigger God who loves each of His children in unique ways.

As mentioned, two individuals scribbled *Graffiti*. In the pages ahead: *street graffiti* is written by my friend, Rick, who lives on the streets. I write *my graffiti* and share thoughts in *heart graffiti*.

My hope, as you read, is that you will find yourself somewhere on the street – his side, my side, or maybe you'll be found standing in the middle. You'll see our stories reflect different scenarios and circumstances, yet there is a sameness to the love exhibited. It's Christ's love that abounds, and that's the story that needs to be told.

While our life stories are intertwined, I leave you with this question: what graffiti has God scribbled on your heart that needs to be told?

Rick's Side of the Street

I came to Corpus Christi, Texas on February 11th, 2011. I had been homeless and on the streets in Houston for a couple of years. With God's nudging, I knew it was time to move on.

Once in Corpus Christi, I was out one evening and ran into the Salvation Army food truck where people were feeding the homeless. This was nothing new to me and I normally would not have been too impressed, but for one thing. These people had brought a large group with them and I got asked at least three times if I needed prayer. Boy did I! So I let the prayer warriors pray. Then one of them handed me a coupon for a free hot dog. I wondered if there was a catch. Yet, it said all I had to do was show up for church one Sunday. No problem – I go to church anyway – and there I'd get my hotdog.

The following Sunday I showed up and went to the service. I went back the next Sunday and noticed they needed some help grilling the hot dogs. So, I jumped in and started cooking the dogs. After grilling awhile, I went inside to the service. It was during praise and worship that I was sure I had seen an angel singing. I might add that to this day she has done nothing to prove me wrong. She sang like an angel and she looked angelic up there under the stage lights.

After the service the Lord led me to share one of my poems with her. I did as the Lord told me. After reciting the poem she did not request a copy, she demanded one! I told her no problem. The next Sunday came around and I gave her the copy and recited another poem. She demanded another copy, and it was given. Those poems have now turned into me unknowingly being part of this book thanks to her urging and constant encouraging.

Writing is something I've been dreaming of doing for years. This angel has been a godsend, to put it mildly. She has got me not only to believe in what God can do through me, but more so to believe in myself. Believing in myself is something I've never done.

I write this introduction with tears of joy running down my cheeks because of the pure joy she brings with every smile and every word. You see, I don't have any physical brothers or sisters and missed out on that part of life, but thank God He brought this wonderful person into my life.

Although I come from the streets, when I needed a cheerleader who believed in me more than I believed in myself, she filled the role perfectly. If I had but one wish it would be that everyone could be blessed by such a person in life because it's makes all the difference in the world.

If you would have told me, years ago, that I would be gifted to write, I would have laughed and quickly told you why that would never happen. First, I don't have a desire to write . . . let alone scribble ANYTHING. Second, English was my worst subject in school and I barely knew a noun from a verb. And third, poetry was for women and sissies – I like to fish and watch football "macho, manly stuff."

Isn't it like God to show up in our weakness and ignorance and change our lives no matter what side of the street we live on or even if we live on the streets?

My Side of the Street

Scribbling out my life's journey I never thought my story was good enough to make a difference, even though I was teaching, speaking, and writing for Christian women. It's crazy how satan paralyzes us in our own journeys.

The more I studied to understand who I was, I actually began to understand more of who God is. I fell in love with His heart and began to feel Him nudging me to reach out and minister to those in need – the abandoned, abused, and homeless. My argument was, how am I going to fit one more thing into my schedule? Not only was I ministering full time, but I was a wife and mom of three teenagers. How was I supposed to find time to minister "outside" the church and better yet how was I supposed to find the abused, abandoned, and homeless? My life was suburban and I was comfortable. I knew God was asking me to give up my "normal" way of thinking and living and I wasn't too sure what would happen.

It was then that my home church began talking of opening up a campus in an old school on the west side of our town, right in the heart of poverty, gangs, drugs, prostitution, and homelessness. My heart skipped a beat the first time I heard of the campus. The thoughts wouldn't let me go. So, I found some courage from within and went. Arriving at that old run-down school, I knew this was home. Every time I left that campus, I had tears in my eyes. I'm not sure about you, but God speaks to me loud and clear through my tears. Oh my, and the tears wouldn't stop.

It didn't take long for God to start showing up in the most incredible ways. Beyond a doubt this community was where God had been preparing me to go for years. With a heart and passion to serve, I stepped out doing whatever I could to bring Christ to broken and hurting souls.

One particular Sunday after singing at all three services, I was exhausted. But there was no way I was going to miss out on my favorite part of being at church – meeting the people and having a moment to share some encouragement. I began walking down the hallway to greet the newcomers and touch base with those who fellowship with us. I wanted to hear how their week had been and how they might need help. I've seen God work miracles in the hallway of that old school and that day was no different.

I noticed there was a man coming quickly towards me. I looked him in the eyes and said with all sincerity, "I'm so glad you are here." He stopped and said, "Thanks for sharing your gift of singing. I have a gift too." At that point I was kind of puzzled as to where our conversation might be going, "Great. I'd love to hear about it."

I watched him. There was something in his eyes that said he had a story. The silence behind his words stopped my heart. He looked like he might have come from the streets, but he was well groomed and spoke with confidence.

"Well, my gift is kind of for girls and sissies." Now my curiosity was really piqued. Part of me wanted to giggle like a schoolgirl, but instead I whispered, "I doubt that." Then a beautiful poem began flowing out of the mouth of this man.

The words penetrated my heart making me think of Jesus... His inflection.... the tone. The sincerity of it all captivated my soul. I wanted to take in every moment. I wanted to remember every word as they were being scribbled on my heart. I wanted that poem!

This man surely had a story to be told. Through my tears, I asked if he could write that poem out for me. I thought I was asking nicely, but maybe somewhere in that moment, I was adamant about getting my hands on that poem, and the gift that had just been shared.

Writing is certainly a gift . . . a gift God had given him and me, even if others didn't understand. I'm in awe of what I've learned through his written words, his past, and his homelessness. If you would have told me years ago that I would be a writer, I too would have quickly told you how there was no way. I remember all too well the glaring red marks all over my English papers. Let's keep it our secret, (Mom, hide your eyes!) but I cheated to pass. I know, I know – you're appalled!

In years past, if you would have told me I'd "do" life with the homeless, I would have quickly asked you, "What are you smokin'?" But as I've learned more, I think God has moved my side of the street closer to the other side of the street. Or maybe today I feel more like I'm standing smack dab in the middle of the street. I'm not sure, but the scribbles on my heart are nothing more than God-inspired.

Through these two stories from different sides of the street, I pray you see God's story. I long for the lines of these pages to inspire you. I want you to realize that the graffiti on your heart comes from all aspects of life and from different sides of the street. It's God's story and the scribbles are heavenly.

Graffiti: Scribbles from Different Sides of the Street is written to challenge you to love and care for those that are abused, broken, and homeless, no matter what side of the street you live on. It's written to challenge you to write your God scribbles down so that others can learn from your journey.

Open your soul and let God begin to paint your heart's graffiti for all to see.

A God-Given Destiny

heart graffiti

Why are we so uncomfortable with those who are different from us? They make us squirm. We scratch our heads. We feel out of place; therefore, they must be wrong because we want to be the standard. But deep down, we all know the truth of the matter; we are all different. We don't want to be different because our hearts cry out "*I want to fit in.*"

True comfort comes when we embrace our unique differences. God creates and forms us the way He sees fit. He places us in the families we're in just the way He wants. He knows our every weakness, trial, and triumph for He prepares the way.

And yet ... we long to be the same because we do not want to stand out. We want to worship the same. We want to believe the same. We want to live in the same neighborhoods. Basically, we want the same opportunities, chances, experiences, and blessings as the next person. I often wonder if we realize what we are asking for.

When nothing is different, there is no difference. How vanilla! For when everything is the same, we experience the same over and over. Talk about mundane! For you and me to leave a mark as difference-makers, we will have to be willing to embrace who we are and be different.

For you to step into the God-given destiny that awaits you, it will take you to realize and to appreciate that *you are different.* You have different gifts, talents, hearts desires, stories and passions.

To really follow Jesus, even if it's to the other side of the street, you will have to be the change maker. You will need to live differently from your friends and sometimes your family.

Letting go of preconceived notions can be scary, but the world is counting on you. *Be different!* Don't let what others consider "being different" derail you, let it empower you.

If you are kind only to your friends,
how are you different from anyone else?
Even pagans do that. (Matt. 5:47 NLT)

Different

street graffiti

As a young boy, I was raised in a very anti-organized religion environment. My father was a functional alcoholic. He taught me to have a good work ethic and treat others with respect. I grew up with a mother who was a rage-a-holic. Basically Dad worked a lot, Mom yelled a lot and I learned a lot. I would lose myself in reading. I would read whatever I could get my hands on. I became an information junkie at an early age. I think this was how I made up for not having any brothers or sisters to play with.

During Mom's fits of rage she would constantly tell me how worthless I was. I can hear her angry words still, *"You'll never – never – amount to anything."* As far back as I can remember this happened on a daily basis. From such an early age, I've never believed in myself. I knew I didn't have anything to offer. It was apparent I was different and useless.

As I approached school age I was excited to attend school. For most children entering first grade can be quite an experience. New school. New friends. New teachers. Everything new. And for me that meant a new country too. My dad was in the oilfield business and my family, all three of us, had just been shipped off to England. As you can imagine it was a very intimidating circumstance to be in.

Finally, the first day of school arrived and I was excited as could be expected. At my new school, uniforms were required, tie and all. Since I had yet to experience the freedom of schools here in the good ole USA, I was undaunted by the strict apparel rules. There was a slight uneasy feeling being the only American in an all-English school. But I was very adaptable and naturally thick-skinned. I was not easily offended.

Learning to play soccer and participating in other English customs were actually a delight in every way for me. You're not very set in your ways at six years old. Life was good, and it was very exciting living in a foreign country. There were sights to see and things to do that most people never get the chance in a lifetime to experience. The weather was cold and wet. That's where the problem reared its ugly head. This was the day I realized I was different.

It had begun raining and with that the raincoats came out. It seems my parents had gotten me everything in the way of the proper uniform except for the uniform raincoat. As the rain poured, I went merrily on my way to school in the traditional yellow slicker. You've seen them. Maybe you had one too. This was a bad answer to the downpour!

Every other school kid had on the uniform brown trench coat. As I arrived, the kids began to laugh and make fun of me. This continued ruthlessly all day. I took the bullying like the six-year old man I was on the outside. But inwardly my feelings were hurt. Returning home that day, I vowed to never attend that school again.

I'm sure this doesn't seem like a big deal to a grown-up but let me assure you that to a six year old it was a dramatic and traumatic experience that has stayed with me for years.

There were lessons to learn that day. Lessons a first-grader couldn't understand, but lessons I internalized as I grew up. Being different hurts.

Even today, being different causes others to question, mock, and avoid me. The Christian world is no exception. Many view me as a freak of nature. The so-called normal society looks at me as a fanatic and overly zealous religious nut case.

But as I reflect back on the little boy who was teased and laughed at because he wore the wrong rain-slicker that dreadful day, I realize that being different isn't a bad thing. Different is defined in the eyes of the beholder. I wasn't like them so they deemed me different. But think about it, if we were all the same, what kind of difference could we make? Not much.

Maybe, just maybe, I was learning at a young age that to make a difference I was going to have to be different. I would dress differently. I would talk differently. I would live differently. I would write poetry. Maybe, just maybe, you need to be different too.

Follow your heart's desire, not the world's. Reach out and love the broken, not condemn them like the world. Embrace the gifts God has given you. Live your life, not theirs. Yes, you too were called to be different on this journey because making a difference means being different.

Mocked by Friends

my graffiti

Growing up in south Texas many would say, hands down, I was different. We were a close family, probably because there was no one else around. My brother, sister and I loved being outdoors. We dug in the dirt, made mud pies, and rode our bikes until our hearts were content or mom called us in for dinner. It was such a peaceful, loving environment.

I had every kind of animal my parents would allow. There were dogs, cats, chickens, ducks, horses, sheep, and cows. It was a dreamland for a girl who wanted to be a veterinarian. With a heart to care for animals, we were always taking in the injured or lost animals that would come across our path. They quickly became part of our family.

Every Sunday morning and evening, we'd venture to church for worship and Bible study. My dad was usually working, but mom made sure we were all dressed neatly and ready to go every week.

The quiet country life was all I knew until I entered school. When I loaded myself onto the big yellow bus that stopped at the end of our long country road driveway I had no idea what school would entail. I soon realized that the students came from everywhere – the country, the city, the rich neighborhoods, and the poverty-stricken streets. And with that came different attitudes. Some students were quiet, shy, and friendly while others were loud, boisterous or a little over-bearing. There's nothing like the education of learning about people. I loved school. Not for the education, but for the friends.

When I was in third grade we had quite a rainy season. I'd get up and prepare for my dad to take me to school. Riding to school with Daddy was so much better than waiting at the bus stop at the end of our long driveway. I loved bundling up and hopping into Daddy's truck. I wouldn't wear a raincoat much to my mother's chagrin. I was weird that way. No raincoats.

One particular day, it was pouring, so Daddy dropped me off as close to the building as he could. He hugged me, kissed me, and sent me on my way. As I neared the building I heard the laughs, snickers, and saw the fingers pointing at me. As I drew closer I could hear the sounds, "Her daddy drives her to school. She's such a baby she has to have a kiss from her daddy." The sneers and comments hurt. They cut to the core. Some of those piercing words were coming out of the mouths of my friends. How could they be making fun of me?

Because at such an early age I had an empathetic heart towards those who were mistreated, I surely couldn't understand how my so-called friends could mock me. I didn't understand why my daddy kissing me good-bye was noteworthy to be ridiculed. Wouldn't every daughter like a daddy who loved and treasured her like my daddy did me? Wouldn't everyone be thankful for a parent who would go out of the way to drive him or her to school when it was raining?

In the days that passed, my mind was comforted by the Bible stories I knew. I remembered learning in class that even Jesus' friends mocked, ridiculed and turned away from him. They spat on Him, making fun of what Jesus knew the truth to be. Jesus took it. He smiled and turned the other cheek. He didn't call down the angels from heaven to take them out. He loved them.

I was thankful I was not spit on, but it was a rude awakening, realizing that being different sometimes hurts. Being different will cause others to turn away. Being different is sometimes necessary.

But the truth was – I did not want to be different.

Broken for Others

heart graffiti

Stepping out of complacency and into a world of the unknown is a freeing step. Scary for sure as you step beyond the familiar, but freeing nevertheless. Are you longing for freedom? If so, then step outside your comfort zone. Come on – it's exhilarating! Let life breathe something new within you.

That liberating feeling you are looking for will be found by stepping outside your comfort zone and into the messy and hurting. Living among the messy, your eyes are no longer drawn to yourself looking for "purpose" and life's calling, but instead your soul is opened to meaning and a hurt that makes you come alive.

Life's meaning can be gathered by helping others and serving them in their place of need. It's a treasure to see more in others than they can see in themselves. A precious gift awaits you if you will but step outside of "normal" and see the world in a new way. I freakishly envisioned life's purpose as big and comfortable with a huge helping of happiness on the side.

But the day I grew tired of the complacent and stepped into the world of unknown to serve and help those who were unknown, I knew it wasn't about a life of being big and comfortable any longer. I found meaning when I began serving and helping the unknown.

What I didn't realize was that when you fall in love with a broken world you become vulnerable – vulnerable to be hurt and crushed. I'm reminded of a quote from Jeff Goins book <u>Wrecked</u>, *"It's hard to get your heart broken on the couch."*

Maybe you've been there:

- you comfort a teenager whose surprise pregnancy ends in abortion
- you lend money to a couple for help only to realize you have enabled their drug problem
- you discipline your strong-willed child only to see the same behavior return

Sometimes it can be frustrating, but underneath the frustration is the way you feel when you sing the blues. Not just a feeling that mellows the heart, but a hurt that makes your heart wonder if being broken for others is worth it.

Being broken for others is hard because it isn't about clean success stories – from rags to riches, from the streets to the skylines. But what I now know is that true purpose and meaning is not clean; it is mostly messy. It's about getting dirty daily with those who are broken, down-and-out, frustrated, depressed, and struggling to find their way. It is about getting dirty so they can become clean.

Living life with meaning hurts sometimes, but I wouldn't have it any other way!

Dear friends, do not be surprised at the fiery ordeal that has come on you to test you, as though something strange were happening to you. But rejoice inasmuch as you participate in the sufferings of Christ, so that you may be overjoyed when his glory is revealed. (1 Peter 4:12-14 NIV)

Words Tear Down

street graffiti

We all remember our first. First love . . . first car . . . first job . . . first poem. What? You don't have a poem. I didn't either until God urged me to get a pen and write. I was a new Christian. To say I was on fire for the Lord is an understatement. This was by far the happiest time of my life.

I had a group I met with every Sunday at church for class. We were active. Most of us were serving God any way we could. We had several times of fellowship weekly and it was at one of these functions that I found myself in my first real spiritual dilemma.

We were eating and enjoying each other's company when I heard a commotion going on in the street outside the house where we were. I went out to see what was going on. I got there just in time to see Bill getting slapped by one of the popular "pretty" girls. She had a friend right behind her. I couldn't believe my eyes. These two otherwise laid-back, easygoing, God-fearing girls were laying into Bill pretty heavily.

I know there are two sides to every story. I knew Bill was unique and sometimes out in leftfield. But he was harmless and I couldn't begin to imagine what had caused this onslaught of verbal rebuke. Knowing Bill as well as I did, I figured he said something off-color, and the situation quickly escalated. But as it turned out, Bill was out of line, but nothing that should have drawn physical reproach.

The girls were out of line, too, and I wasn't sure what to say to them. They had been in church all of their lives. I hadn't. But I knew enough to know that the relationships needed to be mended. As I prayed, I heard a still small voice as plain as day say, "Get a pen."

My excitement grew as I thought God was fixing to give me step-by-step instructions for reconciling my friends. But I was wrong! God gave me a poem. What in the world? How was a poem going to help anybody?

Ignoring the Lonesome

We're in a hurry these days without really caring
Too busy to be loving and sharing.

Only seeing the mountain that we must climb
not slowing down and taking our time.

Seeing a need and saying "why bother"
forgetting the commandment that came from our Father.

Only thinking of things we must do
ignoring the lonesome, neglecting the blue.

Give, because of that gift from above
that precious gift, that gift called love.

Yes, Christ died for you and that's plain to see
but never forget, He also died for me.

As I finished writing down the words I felt God nudging me to take it to the church and read it. Get this . . . in front of the whole congregation. Right!

It was a good thing I was a young Christian and hadn't learned how to argue with God, yet. I took the poem to church the next Sunday evening because that was the smallest crowd. I asked the pastor if I could read it. To my dismay he said "Sure."

With my knees knocking and my stomach churning, I began to feel a little dizzy. Somehow I made my way to the pulpit and began reading the poem. What happened next will never leave my memory. Like a clap of thunder the entire church gave a resounding AMEN! It just about knocked me down. I thought "amens" were reserved for elders and deacons. I quickly returned to my seat.

As the service ended a few folks came to me and were saying how much they liked the poem. Praise I didn't expect. The last two people that came up were the two "pretty" girls with tears rolling down their cheeks. Through the tears I heard, "That poem was about us, wasn't it?" Tearing up I nodded, "yes." I told them how the poem came about as I was praying for reconciliation.

I was glad to see that after that night the two girls went out of their way to make Bill feel like one of the gang. I don't understand why we so carelessly say things that hurt others. People are hurting. People are looking for hope, not cutting words. The broken world needs to hear Christ through the loving and considerate words we speak.

It all starts with the heart. A ghetto heart is full of contempt and ugly comments. A heart set on God is full of love in action and deed. It's time we learn to get our hearts right before anything else. When I began studying the heart, I was very surprised. If how many times something is mentioned in the Bible is any indication of its importance, check out these stats.

Love is mentioned 311 times.
Sin is brought up 448 times.
The heart is written about 833 times.

The heart is spoken of more than love and sin combined.

Proverbs 4:23 NLT says, "Guard your heart above all else, for it determines the course of your life." Is guarding your heart a challenge for you?

Remember the saying; "garbage in, garbage out." Fill your heart with God's Word and peace daily so out of your mouth will flow words that give life instead of tearing it down.

Jail House Rock

my graffiti

Years ago, a woman I barely knew was sent to prison and asked for me to come visit her. It totally took me by surprise. What was this lady thinking? I remember asking, *"Why me, Lord? Why me? Please don't rock my world like this!"*

I had no idea the journey I was about to begin. You see, I'd never been to a prison and I didn't want to go now! In my prayer and quiet time I felt God continually nudging me to go. I kicked and screamed, but finally submitted.

When the day came, I was in a panic. What was I suppose to say to this lady? What would the prison be like? All I could envision was the slamming of the prison doors behind me as I walked in. And to be honest – this freaked me out!

I began begging God to let me out of this assignment, but He didn't relent. He confirmed every step of the way that He was going with me, but that didn't make this journey any easier. Arriving at the prison, a guard confronted me. I had arrived at the wrong time. I had entered the wrong way. He was a gruff man and scared me to death. He finally said, *"Lady, you need to come back in a few hours."*

As I headed back to my car (actually, I was stomping like a two-year old) I was thinking, *"God, this is crazy! I am not coming back here."* And once again He snatched my heart and said, *"Yes you are, child!"* Being the sweet argumentative one that I am, I told God that He had a few hours to prove to me that I should go, as I headed to a fast-food restaurant to get a drink and read my Bible.

Once there, flipping through scripture I came across:

"Then the righteous will answer him, 'Lord, when did we see you hungry and feed you, or thirsty and give you something to drink? When did we see you a stranger and invite you in, or needing clothes and clothe you? When did we see you sick or in prison and go to visit you?' The King will reply, 'I tell you the truth, whatever you did for one of the least of these brothers of mine, you did for me.'" (Matt. 25:37-40 NIV)

As I read that you would think that this would have convinced me, but I once again began to argue with God. *"OK Lord, You say the things we DO are as if we are doing them for You. But if I just don't do it, if I don't go to the prison then what does it hurt? I just haven't done anything for anybody. Right?"* Like God was going to confirm that nonsense. Instead He said, *"Child, keep reading."*

*"They also will answer, 'Lord, when did we see you hungry or thirsty or a stranger or needing clothes or sick or in prison, and did not help you?' He will reply, 'I tell you the truth, whatever you **did not do** for one of the least of these, you did not do for me.'"* (Matt. 25:44-45 NIV)

You can imagine how my heart quickened and my spirit wept when I read the words, **"I tell you the truth, whatever**

you did not do for one of the least of these, you did not do for me." I begged the Lord for forgiveness.

You can probably guess what happened. I traipsed myself back to that prison. This was definitely a jailhouse rock experience for me. God came through in unexpected ways and rocked my way of thinking. I learned that using your gifts, talents, finances, and time for Christ and His cause to reach others will come in ways you least expect it.

My job is to keep my eyes open to how I can unselfishly become the hands and feet of Christ and serve the least of these – the broken, hurting, imprisoned, hungry, grieving, impoverished, abused, addicted, lonely . . .

Opposition to Victory

heart graffiti

Have you been accused of something you didn't do? Are others continually making your life miserable?

To some degree, I think we've all been there at one time. I am continually encouraged as I read through the Psalms, which are mostly written by King David. King David knew that God was fighting for him, and you can know too that God will fight for you.

King David was known as a man after God's own heart, but yet he was so "real." He called it how it was. He shared his "real" feelings with God and asked God to come to his aid. Over and over we see him ask God to change his own heart. What an incredible example for you and me!

If you're struggling, it's time to get your journal out or a piece of paper and write out your own Psalm, your feelings, as a prayer to God. He knows your heart and struggles already. He is just waiting for you to tell Him. As you write your heart-felt concerns out, ask God to come and fight for you.

Then may you hear the Lord say, "I will give you victory!"

O Lord, oppose those who oppose me. Fight those who fight against me. Put on Your armor, and take up Your shield. Prepare for battle, and come to my aid.
Lift up your spear and javelin against those who pursue me.
Let me hear you say, "I will give you victory!"
(Psalm 35:1-3 NLT)

Falsely Accused

street graffiti

The best place to start is always the beginning. This story begins with a girl. Her name was Robbie and she was pregnant. Not with my child, as Robbie was more like a sister I never had, and incest is just not in me.

She came to me in tears and searching for answers. Tough answers like what she was supposed to do with this unborn child. The biological father had already run off and abandoned the situation all together. I was single at the time and had no idea what it was like to face a pregnancy head on, let alone raise a child. My experience in these matters was nil.

The only thing I knew to tell Robbie was that if she decided to keep the child (that was a decision she alone had to make) I would always be there for both her and her baby.

Fast forward, gaze upon the most beautiful thing in the world, her name is Venecia and she is not only my godchild, she is the only child I will ever have. I can't express with mere ink and paper how much I loved, and still do, that baby girl. I was true to my promise and helped raise her.

I finally married and my wife accepted and relished the role of godmother. As Venecia grew up she grew very close to me and it was a very mutual thing. My wife and I were unable to have children and we didn't have the resources to do anything about that. Venecia was our one shot at the kid thing and we both knew it. Life was so good.

Unfortunately things changed over time. My wife and I grew apart and divorce was unavoidable and unwanted, but it resulted just the same. It was during this divorce that my world was shattered and my life forever changed. Not because of the divorce like you might think though, not by a long shot.

I soon learned that friends had a way of siding with the wife. As my friends shunned me, I figured it was because of the divorce and that it would pass when the dust settled. I could not have been more wrong. In one of our last times together I asked my wife why everybody was treating me like I had the plague. What she told me crushed me as a man and as a human being.

She told me that three months earlier Robbie had told everyone that I had molested Venecia. I felt like my gut and heart had literally been ripped from my body. I had been severely abused by my mother and thought I knew what it was like when somebody you love hurts you badly. I didn't have a clue. This made that look like Christmas time with the Walton's.

It is important to note at this time what my house looked like on weekends. It looked like a school. Kids everywhere! Since my wife and I didn't have children of our own, it was agreed by all that we watch someone else's. My wife had a brother with five kids and three sisters with countless amounts of kids. Most of our friends had kids.

Understanding my love for children is what will help you understand my immense pain at the false accusation. With the divorce and being wrongly accused of child molestation my life was over. I was still alive but didn't want to be.

Too chicken for a quick suicide, I proceeded to slowly drink and drug myself to death slowly. I got addicted to crack cocaine, and of course, got all my vitamins from beer. To this day I still don't know how I lived. I wasn't eating or sleeping hardly at all. I was living because of God's grace alone!!

God refused to let me die. I cursed Him at that time for not letting the terrible pain be over.

Years later I ended up back with the Father. Thankful that HE would not give up even though I had. This Father's relentless pursuit of a drunken crack addict had persisted till I finally gave in. Today I understand why He would not give up.

Because of what I have been through, I'm now serving the Lord in a capacity that few could ever do. I help the homeless, destitute, unlovable, forgotten and unwanted. Because of my past pain I now fully understand theirs. Sound familiar? It should!

Our Lord knows all too well what it's like to be in our shoes. He knows all too well what it's like to be falsely accused!

Let Your Secrets Go

my graffiti

Somewhere along my journey of growing up, I decided my story wasn't good enough. I spent many hours trying to duplicate what others were doing. I wanted to act, walk, dress, and talk like them. I wanted to be them!

The notion that my own story was not good or cool followed me into adulthood and marriage. After years of infertility, God blessed my husband and me with three children. I was living my dream of being a stay-at-home mom. But it didn't feel good enough because it was not what my friends were doing. I found myself longing for their stories.

Their lives consisted of being lawyers, doctors, teachers, and nurses. My heart ached because I wasn't content with my own story. It was my dream, so why wasn't it a good enough story?

Years later when God called me to write and speak, I was mortified. I sensed there wasn't much to share because my testimony seemed too boring. Who wanted to hear anything I had to share? I didn't have one of those cool testimonies . . . *rescued from drugs. Removed from an abusive relationship. Found freedom in jail.* My God story didn't even feel good enough!

Shortly thereafter, my husband and I were in the middle of an excruciatingly dark story. We had been scammed by a con artist. We were questioned by the FBI, IRS, and many more. We lost everything. We lost our way. While there was no money and the stress mounted, our marriage almost didn't survive. We were tied up in court with attorneys for 9 years trying to clear our name.

We were wrongly accused by authorities and the evil person who abused us was left roaming free. There it was my story. A story of how we overcame with God's help. But I didn't want to tell anyone. It had shame written all over it. Normal "good girls" aren't questioned by the FBI and IRS. "Good Christian" girls don't get caught up in affairs such as this.

I wanted to run. I hid. I wore a mask. I covered my true hurts until they about broke me. It was then that a friend entered the story of my life and said, "If you let your secrets go, they will have no power over you."

It was that day I decided to let the truth ring out. As time moved on, I had no idea that this story that God had knit together for me would become what I would need to relate to those He put in my path.

My journey soon led me to serve at an inner-city church; a place where I didn't see how I would fit in when I first arrived. I was too white. I was too proper. But as I've been afforded the privilege of speaking, teaching, and ministering there I realize it is the story of my life that gives me a heart to connect with the broken and abused.

It was the truth of my story that I never felt it was good enough that gives me a glimpse into the hearts of how they feel.

While I continually long for purpose, my story seems so insignificant; however, it is certainly the scribbled heart-story God intended me to live out to reach others.

For Your Generation

heart graffiti

Can you feel God stirring newness within your soul? Maybe a holy passion is ringing out and you're not sure how or when to make the change, but you know you must. You want your journey to make a difference.

Looking back, most of my life I've spent intimate time with God praying, "Break my heart FROM what breaks Yours." Maybe that is somewhat like the cry of your prayers too.

God break me FROM – pride, selfishness, gossip, anger, and your list goes on.

You and I long for a heart that is broken FROM and free from sin. But circumstances change when out of nowhere the words of your prayer changes to, "God, break my heart FOR what breaks yours." I wasn't conscious of when my prayer changed, but I can now say it is definitely a scary prayer to pray.

When your heart begins to grasp what God's heart breaks for . . . the broken, homeless, imprisoned, orphaned, widow, prostitute . . . your whole being comes to life with tears, passions, and holy anger. Your life awakens with what your heart beats FOR! What God's heart beats FOR.

Think of King David. He was a man who not only had a heart for God, but also ran his race FOR his generation. Can you imagine what you are called to do for your generation? If so, visualize the lives that can be changed through your obedience.

For your generation – What does your heart beat FOR? Who are you serving? How will others be changed?

Oh please be diligent in fulfilling your complete purpose for which God created you for this generation. Others are counting on you! There's power in that simple prayer, "Lord, break my heart FOR what breaks Yours."

Pray it. Listen in silence. God is calling you out to reach someone in this generation. Will your broken heart go FOR them? Oh, I do hope so.

The day will come when you and I hope to hear the words, "Well done, good and faithful servant!" And I pray we can answer back, "Yes Lord, I served my generation with the purpose that You gave me FOR the people You sent to me!"

"For David…served the purpose of God in his own generation."
(Acts 13:36)

What Would You Do

street graffiti

I was homeless. Not because of drugs or alcohol. Not because I'm lazy and don't want to work. Not because I'm disabled. Not because God didn't care. Quite the opposite.

God cared so much that He placed me in the streets to help. To be a voice for those less fortunate. To take people by the hand and lead them off the streets and hopefully to Jesus.

One day I was in the store and glanced at the newspaper. I noticed an article stating that a homeless man had died of heat stroke. This was especially disturbing as I had implored some people to open a facility and let folks come in and cool off.

It was August in Corpus Christi, Texas and we were going through one of the worst droughts in recorded history. Having lived in south Texas for many years I knew how dangerous this kind of heat could be.

I thought maybe now people would see how dangerous this kind of heat could be and listen. It sometimes takes a tragedy to bring about change. Maybe things would change if the owner of the facility had to come out here for a couple of days.

Years back there was a fad going on in the Christian community where everyone wore bracelets that said, "*What Would Jesus Do?*" While you flaunt your bracelets, t-shirts, and bumper stickers asking those all-important questions, I can say I know what Jesus would do.

The question I leave you is, "what would you do?"

52

What Would You Do? (WWYD)

WWYD . . .

    if you found yourself living on the street

    having to walk miles each day for something to eat?

WWYD . . .

    if the only clothes you have are on your back

    all you are going through is heartache and lack

WWYD . . .

    alone in the world wore out and scared

    thoroughly convinced that nobody cared

WWYD . . .

    when you're constantly being harassed

    you find yourself hopeless and cursing your past

WWYD . . .

    when all you can say to God is, "Why, God? Why?"

    the despair you're feeling makes you want to curl up and
die

WWYD . . .

    your body never ceases to be in pain

    struggling every day and never any gain.

WWYD . . .

    you get drunk to go to sleep at night

    you keep losing no matter how hard you fight

WWYD

    if one day all this was happening to you

    my friend, I know what Jesus would do.

Seeing a Miracle and Injustice

my graffiti

"Mommy, I'm so glad we don't have places like this where we live." Those were the words of one of my children as we wrapped up a week-long mission trip in the projects of Nashville, TN. It had been an amazing week serving children and providing Vacation Bible School (VBS) classes and fun.

I hate to admit it, but this was the first time I had ventured into a ghetto, projects, or impoverished area other than taking day trips across the border into Mexico. How could I have lived so sheltered? Or not ventured out of my own neighborhood and routine? My eyes were opened on this trip and I'll never forget the sounds, smells, and smiles of the children. How did I get there? Did I sign up months in advance eager to go? *Not exactly.*

The youth at our church decided to go to the inner city of Nashville. It happened to be the same week that my children all went to another camp, so we didn't sign up. As time drew near, the trip was short on adult leaders, and they kept calling asking if I'd go. I kept denying the request because my children and I had made our plans, and we were sticking to it.

The week we were to leave for camp, a huge storm flooded most of central Texas. Camp was cancelled for the first time in its history. As the youth leader continued to call me about being an adult leader on this trip, my heart actually began warming to the idea and wondering about this adventure – whatever it might be.

God began bombarding me with the scripture from Isaiah 61. It was everywhere I looked.

> The Spirit of the Sovereign LORD is on me,
> because the LORD has anointed me
> to proclaim good news to the poor.
> He has sent me to bind up the brokenhearted,
> to proclaim freedom for the captives
> and release from darkness for the prisoners,
> to proclaim the year of the LORD's favor.
> Isaiah 61:1-2 NIV

I was actually considering calling and letting them know I'd love to go . . . about the same time I got a call from my daughter. She had blown out her knee in gymnastics practice, so off to the hospital we went.

The youth director didn't give up. He came to visit us and asked one last time if we would go. Seeing my daughter there in pain, I pointed out our obvious situation now. There was no way that knee was going to make it on a two-day drive to Nashville. The youth director said, "I need you to agree to something." Not really sure where this was going, I said "Sure."

He continued. "We are going to pray over this knee for a complete healing. If God chooses to heal it before our trip, you have to go." That sounded like a fair deal to me, but I had major doubts. They were leaving in less than 48 hours and she was in a lot of pain.

The next morning I was in shock. My daughter got out of bed shouting excitedly, "Mom, my knee doesn't hurt. I think it's well!" I couldn't believe what she was saying. It was true, and we had just witnessed a miracle. In my amazement, we all began packing our bags. As I packed, I grew eager in expectation of what I'd learn. What did God have in store? He obviously wanted us there.

The first days serving the community in Nashville were such a blessing. We'd take the bus into the ghetto and gather the children to take back to our facility for VBS. We'd play games and love on all of them. There was this one little girl, LaKesha, who was about 4 years old, and who fell in love with me. She followed me around, holding my hand, and wouldn't leave my sight. She was the most precious little girl, the youngest of her family.

On the third morning as we ventured into the ghetto the children began loading up on the bus one by one. As they filed on I quickly noticed there was no little LaKesha. I continued looking out the window watching for her to come running. I could see her smile and bright eyes in my memory but she never came.

Then out of nowhere the children on the bus started getting rambunctious and talking about the night before. They grew louder and louder:

"Did you see it?"
"It was incredible."
"Yeah. He drug her for about a mile."
"Who?"

"You didn't see it."
"That drug dealer ran right over her."
"It was awesome. He drug her around the block."
"Where is she?"
"LaKesha is in the hospital."

I turned around. "What?" It seemed like the children all screamed in unison at that moment, "Miss, they ran over LaKesha. It was bad." My heart screamed. I wanted to pound somebody. The injustice of it all was crazy. And the children . . . they talked about it like this incident was something that happened every day. As I sat and listened, I learned LaKesha had died that dreadful evening. I heard the children laughing and shouting, as if nothing out of the ordinary had just happened. My heart could barely handle the moment.

The rest of the week I spent ranting to God. "Why did you call me here? I open my heart to a hurting world and now I'm crushed. I can't make a difference. I don't see how anybody can make a difference in these situations. It's the ghetto. It's their heart. It's all so hopeless. LaKesha is dead."

I'm not sure if you're questioning God and what He can do through you, but I can truly say, "it's no use." Even in the midst of your questions, doubt, and struggle God can still do miracles. All He needs is someone willing to step out and go. Whether you go to the ghetto, the suburbs, another country, your church, or the street corner, God can work through you as long as you are obedient. Listen . . . do you hear His call?

You might want to rant. You may rave. You will probably have many questions and need answers. You will cry your eyes out and bang your fists at some of the injustices, but keep working for God and He will work through you to reach a hurting world.

Silence Births Vision

heart graffiti

Have you had those seasons where you felt God was silent? Maybe you are there now. You seek and search, yet no answer. You might feel Him stirring and moving your heart, but no real breakthrough.

Silence is Oh. So. Awkward. Reflecting on the Christmas season you see periods of silence. And immediately your mind is drawn to:

Silent Night, Holy Night,
All is Calm, All is Bright

I'm not sure how silent, holy, calm and bright those days were leading up to Christ's birth. When you reflect on the years before the night our Savior was born, you learn:

- Christ was born after a period of silence! 400 years of silence. God was silent as the world waited for the Messiah.
- As the world awaited a Savior, the silence resonated of new beginnings, new life, and yet something unfamiliar was about to happen.
- Before the silence was broken with the birth of Jesus, He was there. Although unseen He was – moving, speaking, stirring, and preparing.

As we sense silence in our lives, we just have to know that God is preparing to do a new and incredible thing in our lives. We need to hold on, stay in His presence, and prepare.

Although we're not comfortable with silence, we must hang on to the fact that God speaks in the quietest of whispers. And for you and me to hear the softest of whispers of God, we need silence.

Every year as Christmas approaches, I find myself longing for the quiet. Oh how hard it is to find. The busyness of the world and the holiday season make it almost impossible. Our world screams even louder at that time of year "buy it – get it – it's all about you and what you want."

But what if we were to silence those thoughts this season? To hear what Jesus would long to whisper to our souls, that the Christ child was born to do something new in each of our lives. My heart is saddened to think I might miss what the Savior wants to say and do within me.

I pray through the silent lines of this book that the Lord has unveiled the silence within you and given birth to a new direction and vision. I want these scribbles to touch your soul and help you see how powerful your quiet journey is to furthering the Kingdom.

While all is silent and calm, will you listen for the voice of a Savior, coming to your side of the street?

His Love

street graffiti

Jingle Bells. Jingle Bells.
Dashing through the snow.
Bright colored lights. Children laughing.
Ho. Ho. Ho.

It was Christmas Eve and I was at a party. Unfortunately, it was a pity party. There was no tree, no presents, no children, no wrapping paper flying, and no family. There was me sitting alone – sulking.

I woke up that morning at a homeless shelter - the Men's Center in Houston, Texas. I was finally sober and had a lot to be thankful for, but I couldn't see that at the time. It is hard to see clearly through a veil of contempt.

As I contemplated my situation, my thought pattern was interrupted. My attention was drawn to the television when the Gatlin Brothers started singing a wonderful song about how Jesus was the reason for the season. We've heard that a million times, but that night I understood it personally. My spirit started to brighten as I began to focus on how much I had been given, instead of what I lacked. A feeling of immense gratitude came over me as tears came to my eyes.

I had a lot to be thankful for – a year of sobriety, great health, and wonderful new friends. I started thanking God for His presence and all that He had done. But mostly that evening, I was thankful for His love and the peace that He had brought me. I wanted to share this abundantly peaceful feeling with others. Others on the streets needed this.

To my delight, as God pulled me out of my pity party, He provided a great gift. Sitting alone in the shelter with a thankful spirit beautiful words of poetry began to flow.

His Love

When anxious, worried, and full of strife
When all you can say is "why my life!"
Remember . . . His love was always there.
When troubles come and you think, *not again!*
When you lose a battle you were sure you'd win
Remember . . . His love was always there.
When relentless temptation is at every turn
When thoroughly convinced you'll never learn
Remember . . . His love was always there.
When tired, down trodden, and feel like giving up the fight
When it turned out wrong and you just knew it was right
Remember . . . His love was always there.
When He came to earth merely a man – flesh and bone
When so unselfishly He gave to make us His own
Remember . . . His love was always there.
When beaten and bloody, wrongly hung on a tree
When dying for people like you and like me
Remember . . . His Love will always be here.

That Christmas Eve as I sat angry, lonely, and troubled, God showed up with a gift. It wasn't wrapped in pretty paper with a bow, nor found perfectly placed under a brightly lit tree. No, it was placed directly into my broken heart.

As the years passed and I hit hard times on the streets it was the gift of "His Love" that kept me going. The only perfect gift is Jesus! No packages. No bows. Just Jesus. The gift of a poem from God is incredible, but the ultimate gift is the reminder of His presence and His Love.

All I Want

my graffiti

It was that time of year when the all too familiar words "All I Want" were heard from young and old alike.

Mommy, all I want for Christmas is . . .
Hubby, all I want is . . .
Santa, all I want is _____ . . .

I'm not sure how you would fill in the blank, but after meeting another sojourner from a desperate side of the street, I have a new perspective for the words "all I want."

The weather was quite drizzly, cold, and windy. As I was leaving the church building one afternoon, a homeless man who had been visiting came in out of the cold and we began to chat. In the course of our conversation, he downheartedly said, "All I want . . ."

I'm not sure how you think he might have finished that sentence, but my heart was taken back by his words. "All I want is a tarp to cover what little stuff I have that is now getting ruined by this rain."

Oh friends, while we were thinking of all the things we wanted to fix up and fill our homes with for the holiday season, there this man stood with only a few items to call his own. All he was wishing for was a tarp so he'd have a dry place to lay his head and protect his "stuff."

As we create our lists and check them twice, there are some people reflecting on the true meaning of Christmas and wondering if it will never dwell within their hearts, not to mention a home. And you and I stay busy with our hustling and busting, not seeing the true meaning of giving.

I'm not sure why there is the disconnect. I guess it could be a number of things. Why we let Mr. Grinch steal the true Christmas spirit is still a mystery.

We each know deep down that Christmas doesn't happen in the form of packages, boxes or bags. It happens in the realm of giving to children, men and women. Christmas doesn't happen because your house finally gets decorated and the boxes neatly wrapped. No, it happens when we are out loving on those who wondered if Christmas would even come.

Christmas comes in the form of hugs from children, sticky candy on the floor, and smiles as big as Texas from those receiving gifts. Christmas comes to those who can say, "All I want is to help another have Christmas." Christmas comes to those who only long for a tarp in the rain.

This season, all I want for Christmas is the joy of smiling faces knowing that the real joy of Christmas didn't come in packages, boxes, or bags!

Concluding Graffiti

I pray you've seen yourself amid the graffiti and street talk. It's an incredible journey when we realize there is so much to be learned from the stories . . . even the stories that come from another side of town or a different street.

Recently, I piled into a car with a few friends to travel a few miles down the city strip to give sandwiches and cool water to the homeless congregated downtown under the shade trees. The streets were quiet. There wasn't a soul stirring.

Finding a spot to park, we unloaded a cooler full of water and set up a little folding table to put the bagged lunches on. A few men walked by and we'd wave them over "Are you hungry?" An "Oh, yes," seemed to be the usual response. We visited, prayed, and asked if they needed anything. There was a sweet aroma of love in the air. I found myself feeling at home on this side of the street. The heart stories amazed me continually.

As I handed out lunch, I found myself in conversation with a dear woman, and as our conversation ended, she turned to leave. I was captivated by her heart and quickly called after her, "Ma'am – can I pray with you?"

With the most precious toothless grin, her blue eyes looked into mine and she said, "Yes, but I want to pray. Is it alright, because I only know one prayer?"

I nodded. We bowed our heads and she began *"Our Father . . ."*

Tears flowed freely down my cheeks as my heart connected with hers. It was as if the graffiti of our souls was becoming blurred and smudged. All of a sudden, the bold outlines of the art of our lives didn't matter. Even the street where we stood was common ground.

. . . *"who art in heaven, hallowed be Thy name; Thy kingdom come; Thy will be done on earth as it is in heaven. Give us this day our daily bread; and forgive us our trespasses as we forgive those who trespass against us; and lead us not into temptation, but deliver us from evil. For the kingdom, the power, and the glory are Yours now and for ever. Amen."*

Maybe there is something to standing in the middle of the street realizing that there's more common ground there than on the sides of the street. This is the beautiful graffiti of the heart, of which life is made, if we can only open our eyes and see. To see not the bold outlines and colors that make us different, but to see the heart graffiti that makes us the same.

Thank you to my friend, my brother, who lives down the street and under a mesquite tree, for your beautiful scribbles of graffiti! You've taught me to be brave and step across the street, to see that although our streets are different our hearts are the same, and you've taught me to be bold and write God's graffiti out for all to see.

My challenge to you: Live your life out with bold colors of graffiti. Share your side of the street with another to find common ground. Scribble out your God story to encourage another.

About the Author

Alene Snodgrass is a motivational writer, speaker and teacher who loves to tell the untold story. She speaks around the country at conferences, retreats, and women's groups sharing Christ through her real life experiences. She is the author of *Dirty Laundry Secrets – a Journey to Meet the Launderer* and *I'm a Fixer-Upper – A Day-by-Day Remodeling Guide.*

Alene has been published in numerous books, writes for *WHOA Magazine* and leads online studies. Alene, her husband, two daughters, son and daughter-in-law reside in Corpus Christi, Texas. You can visit her at www.positivelyalene.com or email alene@alenesnodgrass.com.

To connect with Alene, visit her at the following:

Email: alene@alenesnodgrass.com
Blog: www.positivelyalene.com
Facebook: Alene Snodgrass
Twitter: https://twitter.com/AleneSnodgrass

More about Graffiti

Website: http://www.graffitithebook.com/
Download the *Graffiti: Study and Do guide.*

What Do You Do Now

You've finished reading *Graffiti* and you know there is more. There is always more to the story, right? Well, there is. You now have three choices:

1. You can share this book with others. Share what you liked and what you didn't like. Share what inspired you and what made you feel uncomfortable.
2. You can share your thoughts with me. I'd love to know what thoughts resounded through your soul as you read.
3. You can share your story. I love to help others tell their untold story. You can tell it bravely as yourself or you can tell it anonymously. Either way your heart graffiti needs to be told to encourage others on their journey.

To submit a story or share your thoughts, email me at alene@alenesnodgrass.com.

Download the Study and Do guide and read other untold stories by visiting http://www.graffitithebook.com/.

More Resources for Your Journey

Jennie Allen, *Anything: The Prayer that Unlocked My God and My Soul*, (Thomas Nelson, Inc. 2011) -- http://jennieallen.com/

Seth Barnes, *Kingdom Journeys: Rediscovering the Lost Spiritual Discipline*, (Ashland Press 2012) -- http://www.sethbarnes.com/

Jeff Goins, *Wrecked: When a Broken World Slams into Your Comfortable Life*, (Moody Publishers, New Edition, 2012) -- http://goinswriter.com/

Jen Hatmaker, *Interrupted: An Adventure in Relearning the Essentials of Faith*, (NavPress 2009) -- http://jenhatmaker.com/

19576848R00040

Made in the USA
Charleston, SC
01 June 2013